GARY SCHOCKER
Flute Pieces with Piano

PLAYBACK+

Speed • Pitch • Balance • Loop

To access audio, visit:
www.halleonard.com/mylibrary

Enter Code
8123-3512-6588-1065

ISBN 978-1-59615-814-6

Music Minus One

EXCLUSIVELY DISTRIBUTED BY

HAL•LEONARD®

Visit Hal Leonard Online at
www.halleonard.com

World headquarters, contact:
Hal Leonard
7777 West Bluemound Road
Milwaukee, WI 53213
Email: info@halleonard.com

In Europe, contact:
Hal Leonard Europe Limited
1 Red Place
London, W1K 6PL
Email: info@halleonardeurope.com

In Australia, contact:
Hal Leonard Australia Pty. Ltd.
4 Lentara Court
Cheltenham, Victoria, 3192 Australia
Email: info@halleonard.com.au

CONTENTS

Foreword

DANCES AND DAYDREAMS

These pieces are somewhat less technically difficult than a lot of my other music. But they are musically sophisticated, and require careful listening between the players.

gallant This is a Schubert-induced parlor piece. Play it with charm and humor, enjoying the little grace notes, which can tug at the heart. The little excursion into minor is a surprise. The best way to accomplish surprise in music is to react after something happens rather by preparing and underlining the particular moment. This will create more a feeling of creation rather than planned and enforced playing. Keep the cuckoo sounding light and happy at the end.

in the library is more introspective than the first movement. I called it this because it sounds like the emotion is strong but being kept carefully quiet. Although there is considerable brightening before the recapitulation, the piece ends darkly, echoing the cuckoo call of the first movement, this time in a more serious mood.

sarabande is based on the baroque dance movement. Enjoy the descending 7ths, and ascending 6ths, and feel free to be especially expressive in those spots. Trills always sound faster if the speed is kept constant from the very first shake.

rainbows an ascending octave connotes great longing in the language of music. Perhaps the most famous example is in the classic Harold Arlen song *Over the Rainbow*, which marries the perfect words to that particular musical expression. The middle part is caused by subtle changes in the piano part, leading the music inward. The theme is hinted at only again, and then dissolves—like a rainbow.

pilgrims has a baroque feel at the beginning, changing to a jazzier rhythm in the middle,. Then the two styles are briefly traded back and forth before the opening melody comes back, and disappears suddenly.

sicilienne keep a feeling of airy lightness at all times, riding along on the rhythm of the piano part. Experiment with playing with less *vibrato* to make a more baroque sound at times.

spring energy Lots of happy music here, reminiscent of old English song. The little mini-trills are meant to be humorous. Bring out any clashes, rather than downplaying them. Pay attention to all the dynamic shifts, which add color to this movement.

early one morning try for a fresh clear tone, as the title suggests. Float the high notes, avoid too much *vibrato* for a clear tone.

largo means long. The idea is to lengthen the notes, creating a feeling of floating; this movement must not rush forward. Instead, visualize of a hot air balloon as an image for how a largo moves. The surprise modulation through g# minor to B major requires a color change from the rich tone appropriate for the opening. The piece ends mysteriously without resolution in the final piano chord to a pure G-major chord.

Istanbul Here you can experiment with a more unusual sound to try and create an exotic atmosphere. The flute can play with placement of the fast notes, bunching them a little tighter than marked, to make the part sound more improvised. Hold back on *vibrato* to alter the colors. The trills sound more like cries if they have sudden crescendos in them.

holà! is an upbeat dance, Latin style. The mood is happy. Keep the tone buoyant, not heavy and pay attention to the marking and accents to bring charm to the piece. In the middle section remember that an eighth is always an eighth and just play through the bars without resetting for the metric changes by doing any squeezing or pulsing in the body.

FROM MY JOURNAL

is a soliloquy; imagine a character in a film, alone, just before entering a scene with others. We know what is in their mind, which draws us to them as we watch them in the ensuing scene. For the high g# stay steady—don't take an extra big breath, which will probably make the note heavy and dull.

NATIVE AMERICAN SUITE

This music has many clashes in it, and it is important to celebrate them. Don't be timid when you hear the flute is fighting the chords in the piano. It is preferable to push against the notes that feel wrong. That way, the resolutions will be more beautiful. In other words, playing needs to be ugly in order to be beautiful, at times.

The first movement has many such clashes. Stress the notes that seem not to fit, and recognize the feeling of frustration and anguish in the music.

The second part has the most typically Native American Indian feel. It's fun to imitate a wooden flute by playing some of the intervals a little out of tune, not always measured and perfect. As long as you come back to level tuning, a note here and there that is stretched up will only serve to pique the curiosity of the listening ear. Don't be alarmed by metric changes. One important thing I try to teach is to sense the beat, rather than pulsing in the spine or, worse yet, tapping the foot. Imagine where the beat goes, and let it be continuous through the meter changes, rather than stopping to reset, accenting downbeats in bars which are in new time signatures.

Third Movement requires a limpid liquidity in the top register. This is primarily achieved by keeping the ribs and spine the same as they would be in the lower and middle registers, rather than hiking them up to "support," which causes harshness and out-of-tune playing. Better to think of pushing the air faster. This sometimes can be accomplished by imaging blowing the air down from your nose rather than blowing from front to back through the body.

Last Movement is a joyous dance, and needs to be played with abandon. It should feel like you are having fun, not trying so hard to make little pieces fit together. Try the du-ckee tonguing here at times and see if it frees things up. Also, see whether you are changing the tongue position while tonguing from when there is *legato* playing, which can cause sluggishness. The tongue will not be pushed. It must be released into speed like a gyroscope.

REGRETS AND RESOLUTIONS

was commissioned to celebrate Mortimer Levitt's 80th birthday. It seemed such a milestone birthday would include some looking back, maybe seeing other ways those 80 years could have been spent. That is the *Regrets* movement. This gives way to the forward-thinking resolutions which are more joyous, and although theirs is a look back over the shoulder, this time the mood is more optimistic and the theme, which had been previously curtailed by five chords in the piano, is allowed to blossom and develop in another way.

Sometimes, because the language here is accessible and melodic, I have heard people change notes, add slides, etc. This is completely against my wishes. I am very specific, and do not encourage improvisation in my music. Rather, the feeling of improvisation occurs when a player opens themselves to the emotions that surface while playing, and allow the piece to be whatever the piece is for them in the moment, rather than deciding beforehand by adding swells, or *ritardandi*, or any sort of premeditated thing. For me, music is not about doing things; rather, ideas occur to me while I play and I try and let them float out of my flute in a free-associative way. This way, each performance can be unique.

Technically: try sometimes articulating du-ck-ee instead of te-ke or du-ge. It is a very clean way to play fast, even sixteenths. Of course, it is best not to use one articulation all the time, which will dull the listener's ear.

GREEN PLACES

is a concerto for flute and chamber orchestra, heard here in the flute/piano version. The piece was commissioned by Sir James Galway who gave the premiere at the Adair Festival in Ireland and the US premiere with the New Jersey Symphony.

There are three different depictions of gardens. The first, *Topiary*, is a formal clipped garden in the form of a maze. At its center is a strange place, much less formal and other worldly. While composing this part the words "what is this strange place where blue flowers grow on the cinnamon trees" flashed through my mind, and I set the opening phrase of the B section to those words.

Nightblooming is a serene scented garden where jasmine, tuberose, moonflowers and queen-of-the-night blossom and share their perfumes.

Trollgarden is a wild ride through a craggy wood, with a glance over the shoulder at the topiary garden now in the distance.

ARIRANG

is a well-known Korean folk melody, here in my arrangement for flute. Start with a woody, reedy sound for the opening solo bars. Play the melody simply with personal expression being more important than a polished tone. When I breathe, I avoid pulling up. Instead, the breath seems to come in at body level all-around, rather than being pulled down my throat, which tightens the physical mechanism. Try to take less breath; usually grabbing at breath just causes muscle tightness and the result is less air, not more. I like to cross my right index finger over to play the last trill, instead of using the usual left hand finger for the job. Just be careful not to grip the flute when you cross the hands, which could roll the *embouchure* in and change the tuning.

AT NIGHT

r u sleeping was written for my good friend Fred Marcusa. We often get together and compare flutes. This piece was a thank you to Fred for selling me a remarkable Louis Lot.

The piece, like all the pieces in this set, is intimate. Do not play loud. Instead look for as many shades of *p* and *mp* as you can find. The parts must dovetail, so the pianist needs to sense the same rhythmic flow. Again—resist the urge to beat or pulse. Let the music flow. Part of the joy of playing along with a recording is being able to nestle into a pre-made rhythmic cocoon. Trust your own rhythmic instincts. The piece should sound as the title suggests: you are asking someone whether they are sleeping or not—gently so as not to wake them in case they are indeed asleep.

Sultry Night Short phrases should be played with a kind of jazz-tinted breathiness, rather than a full-flung operatic *vibrato*. It should feel improvised. The piece is a kind of freefall *bossa nova*.

Darkened Room This is a nocturnal piece as well. It is the most dramatic and fulsome of the three pieces. It has the feeling of a soliloquy, more accompanied this time by the piano than in dialogue as earlier. Again, here the high notes must have clarity and distinction and never sound forced. Keep the ribs and spine loose and do not pull up for the high notes. Believe it or not, sometimes it can help to actually go up on your toes. This way, the ribs cannot easily pull up so the body stays more in its natural composed alignment.

SCHERZO

was my first published piece. After attending Julius Baker's master class in 1975 when I was 15, I came home full of ideas and determination, both of which can be heard in abundance here. The articulation will be cleaner if you do not try to force the tongue. Try to release the sides of the back of the tongue instead of always tonguing from the tip, which can cause a small tight sound. Again—variety is the key here. The body does not like to do the same thing over and over.

The high D can be played with the usual fingering, or try b-flat thumb and D key in the right hand (nothing else). The D pops out quite easily and is less sharp this way. I use both fingerings, depending upon the particular pattern.

If your flute is prone to cracking on the middle E, you might try also putting down the c# along with the d# key, which can clarify that note on some flutes. I am suggesting this for notes at the beginning of a phrase, rather than trying to grab all those keys all the time.

IN MEMORIAM

was written for two friends who died the same year, and was the first classical piece I wrote as an adult. It was originally for solo piano. The first part is a picture in the present. The second verse is a memory of childhood, and then finally in some kind of afterlife.

Weave through the rocking rhythm of the piano, allowing for an easy *rubato* without slowing down the tempo.

—*Gary Schocker*

The printed piano accompaniment parts for the pieces in this album

are available from

Theodore Presser Company

www.presser.com

Dances and Daydreams
(11 Pieces for Flutists of All Ages)
for Flute and Piano

Flute

GARY SCHOCKER

I. Gallant

8

II. In the Library

III. Sarabande

IV. Rainbows

X. Istanbul

XI. Holà!

Flute

From My Journal
for Flute and Piano

GARY SCHOCKER

Flute

Native American Suite
for Flute and Piano

GARY SCHOCKER

1. Incantation
Lento (♩=c.66)

2. Spirit Dance
Moderato (♩=c.84)

3. Hidden Spring
Andante (♩=c.66-69)

4. Harvest Time
♩=c.152

* ⌣ optional slurs

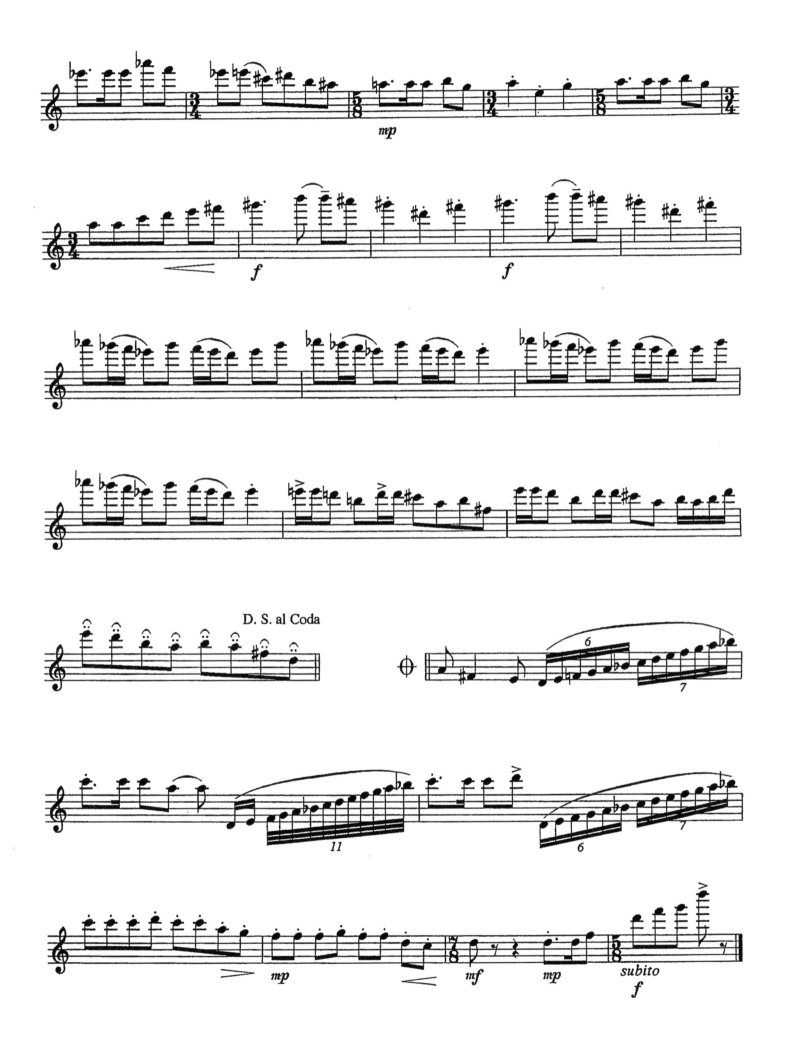

Regrets and Resolutions
for Flute and Piano

Flute

GARY SCHOCKER

for James Galway

Green Places

for Flute and Chamber Orchestra

Flute

GARY SCHOCKER
(1992)

I. Topiary

This page was intentionally left blank to facilitate page turns.

II. Nightblooming

III. Troll Garden

Flute

Arirang
for Flute and Piano

KOREAN FOLK SONG
Arranged by Gary Schocker

* For a particularly effective non-vibrato tone, try this fingering: LH fingers T 2 4,
RH1 plays first trill key, RH2 fingers E key, and RH4 fingers C key.

for Fred Marcusa
At Night

Three Nocturnes for Flute and Piano

GARY SCHOCKER

1. r u sleeping?

2. Sultry Night

3. Darkened Room

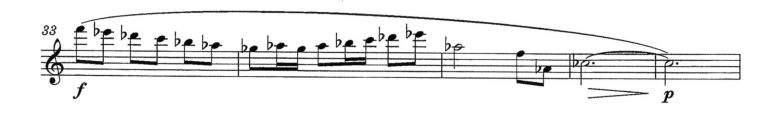

for Julius Baker

Scherzo
for Flute and Piano

GARY SCHOCKER

Flute

♩ = 120–126

August 1975

Flute

for my father, Paul

In Memoriam

for Flute and Piano

GARY SCHOCKER

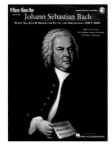